DATE DUE

RUTHERFORD B.
HAYES

PRESIDENTIAL ✦ LEADERS

RUTHERFORD B. HAYES

DEBBIE LEVY

TWENTY-FIRST CENTURY BOOKS/MINNEAPOLIS

For my mother, Jutta S. Levy

Twenty-First Century Books
A division of Lerner Publishing Group
241 First Avenue North
Minneapolis, MN 55401 U.S.A.

Website address: www.lernerbooks.com

Library of Congress Cataloging-in-Publication Data

Levy, Debbie.
    Rutherford B. Hayes / by Debbie Levy.
        p.   cm. — (Presidential leaders)
    Includes bibliographical references and index.
    ISBN-13: 978-0-8225-1493-0 (lib.bdg. : alk. paper)
    ISBN-10: 0-8225-1493-1 (lib.bdg. : alk. paper)
        1. Hayes, Rutherford Birchard, 1822-1893—Juvenile literature. 2. Presidents—United States—Biography—Juvenile literature. I. Title. II. Series.
    E682.L485 2007
    973.8'3092—dc22   2005032494

Manufactured in the United States of America
1 2 3 4 5 6 – JR – 12 11 10 09 08 07

CONTENTS

———— ✧ ————

DEMOCRATS

'PUT UP'

OR

SHUT UP

I Want to BET From

$100 to $500!

THAT R. B. HAYES

Will be elected President of the United States of America. The money is now deposited at the office of the HERALD AND UNION.

Nov. 6th, 1876.   **GEORGE MARLETTE.**

A Republican voter advertised his belief that Rutherford B. Hayes would win the 1876 presidential election.

INTRODUCTION

PRESIDENCY IN THE BALANCE

[S]oon we began to feel that Ohio was not doing as well as we had hoped. The effect was depressing.
—Rutherford B. Hayes, describing
election night, 1876

On election day, November 7, 1876, Republican presidential candidate Rutherford Birchard Hayes spent the evening with family and friends. Gathered in the parlor of Hayes's Columbus, Ohio, home, they learned that his Democratic opponent, Samuel Tilden, had won a majority of votes in New York, New Jersey, Connecticut, and Indiana. After serving refreshments, Hayes's wife, Lucy, went to bed. Hayes joined her shortly after. Certain of his loss, Hayes later wrote in his diary that "the affair seemed over."

Not all Republicans went to sleep that election night, however. In New York, Republican politician General

Daniel Sickles stopped by the city's Republican headquarters and read the incomplete election returns. Tilden seemed to be winning the entire South, which gave him enough votes to win the election. But the results were not final, and they were not entirely reliable. Sickles realized that if South Carolina, Louisiana, and Florida went for Hayes, then Hayes could win. Sickles sent telegrams to Republican leaders in the three states. "Hold your state," he commanded.

Another New Yorker, John Reid of the *New York Times*, also worked late on election night. He came to the same realization as Sickles. A fervent Republican, Reid immediately got in touch with other New York Republican leaders. They sent another round of telegrams to Republicans in the key states, telling them that Hayes's election depended on them.

The next morning, November 8, Hayes—then governor of Ohio—went to his office as usual. As the day progressed, rumors of his victory spread among his supporters in Columbus. That evening, a throng gathered outside his house offering congratulations. Based on their count of the ballots in South Carolina, Louisiana, and Florida, his supporters were claiming victory. But Tilden's Democratic supporters had made their own counts, and they, too, were claiming victory for their candidate.

Thus began one of the bitterest conflicts in the history of U.S. presidential elections. The dispute dragged on for days and then weeks. An inauguration (swearing-in ceremony) was scheduled to take place in Washington, D.C., on March 5, 1877, but no one was certain who would become the nineteenth president of the United States.

CHAPTER ONE

GROWING UP

*I do not think I shall have to go home because
I am homesick. I like staying here better than
any other school in Ohio.*
—thirteen-year-old Rutherford Hayes's first
impressions of boarding school

By the time the leaves dropped from the trees in the autumn of 1822, Sophia Birchard Hayes had endured enough unhappiness for one woman. When Sophia was a girl growing up in Vermont, her father had died, followed by her sister, brother, and mother. Later, Sophia married a Vermont shopkeeper, Rutherford Hayes Jr. They moved to Ohio in September 1817, settling in the central Ohio village of Delaware, near the city of Columbus. There they bought a farm. By 1821 the young Hayes family had three children, Lorenzo, Sarah, and Fanny. Sophia's losses began again. First little Sarah died. Then, in July 1822, Rutherford died suddenly. At thirty years old, Sophia was the single mother of two young children and seven months pregnant.

On October 4, 1822, Sophia gave birth to a sickly baby boy and seemed headed for one more jolt of sorrow. The feeble baby appeared likely to die. Sophia named him Rutherford Birchard Hayes, after his father.

SHELTERED CHILDHOOD
Rutherford, called Rud or Ruddy, was weak and unhealthy. His mother feared for his life and watched him anxiously.

——————————————— ✧ ———————————————

Rutherford B. Hayes was born in this brick farmhouse in 1822.

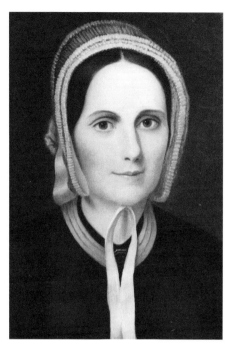 

Sardis Birchard (right) helped his sister Sophia (left) raise her young children.

———————————————— ✧ ————————————————

Although Sophia no longer had a husband, she was not alone in looking out for little Rud and her other children. Living with her in an unfinished brick house that her husband had begun building before his death were Sophia's younger brother, Sardis Birchard, and her cousin, a young woman named Arcena Smith. Sardis and Arcena helped Sophia take care of her family, house, and farm.

Despite his mother's fears, Rud did not die. But Sophia's worries were met with another unexpected tragedy. In January 1825, while skating on a millpond, Rud's older brother, Lorenzo, fell through the ice and drowned. He was nine years old.

After Lorenzo's death, Sophia hardly let Fanny and Rud out of her sight. They were not allowed to play with other children, for fear of accidents, disease, or other disaster. So Fanny and Rud turned to each other for friendship.

HAPPY DAYS

Rud remained weak as a young boy, so Fanny served as caretaker as well as friend. Later he wrote, "My earliest recollection of Fanny is as my protector and nurse when I was a sickly, feeble boy, three or four years old. She would lead me carefully about the garden and barnyard and on short visits to the nearest neighbors. She was loving and kind to me and very generous."

A grateful Rud returned Fanny's love and care. When she became seriously ill in 1827, he amused her during her long recovery period. "I daily gave her little rides upon a small hand-sled which with great difficulty I hauled about the garden," he wrote later. "We were both very happy."

Happiness and well-being soon became the main features of young Rud's life and personality. The Hayes family did not have a great deal of money, but Rud and Fanny were not deprived. Their uncle Sardis Birchard was involved in every aspect of the children's upbringing. A successful merchant and land dealer, he contributed substantially to the family finances. In 1827 he moved farther north in Ohio, to the town of Lower Sandusky, but he remained deeply involved in Rud and Fanny's lives.

LOVING LIFE

By the time Rud was eight years old, he had grown healthy and strong. He was good looking, with blues eyes and light brown hair. He was naturally high-spirited, and his mother often had to correct his manners and tell him to quiet down. Less fearful about her children's health, Sophia lifted her rule against playing with other children. Still, Rud's best friend remained his sister, Fanny. They joked constantly, played, and frequently had fistfights—only to become best friends again.

Rud and Fanny also began to attend the new public school in Delaware. According to Rud, "The school was free to all and was crowded with scholars of all ages, from little folks of our own size up to young men grown." Rud also observed that schoolmaster Daniel Granger was "a little, thin, wiry, energetic Yankee [New Englander]. . . . He threw a large jack-knife, carefully aimed so as just to miss, at the head of a boy who was whispering near me. All the younger scholars were horribly afraid of him. We thought our lives were in danger. We knew he would kill some of us." In fact, the schoolmaster never hurt any of his students and was known to the adults of Delaware as a kind man.

Rud's life as a sheltered, sickly boy was clearly over. Despite his years of isolation from other children, Rud was outgoing and friendly. He loved his life, his hometown, his state, and his country. His sister, mother, Uncle Sardis, and cousin Arcena all showered him with love and encouragement, which helped him grow into a self-confident adolescent.

EARLY TRAVELER
In the summer of 1834, eleven-year-old Rud and his family traveled to New England, home of their ancestors,

where many relatives still lived. Rud enjoyed all the different modes of transportation used on the trip, from old-fashioned stagecoach to brand-new railroad, from river steamboat to canal boat on the Erie Canal. He enjoyed visiting such unfamiliar places as a paper mill, a sawmill, and an ironworks. In Vermont, New Hampshire, and Massachusetts, he enjoyed meeting his relatives and playing with his younger cousins. "I had lots of fun," he wrote in a diary he started around this time, "with George [a cousin] breaking up bumblebees' nests."

Rud took to traveling so well that back in Ohio, Sophia allowed him and Fanny to travel by stagecoach, on their own, to Lower Sandusky to visit Uncle Sardis. Soon after that trip, when Rud was thirteen, his uncle and mother

───────────────── ✦ ─────────────────

Rud and Fanny may have ridden in a stagecoach similar to this one when they went to visit Uncle Sardis on their own in 1834.

realized that the teenager had outgrown the educational opportunities in his hometown. Sardis and Sophia wanted Rud to attend a more advanced school to prepare him for college. Sardis proposed the Norwalk Seminary in Norwalk, Ohio, an all-boys' boarding school thirty miles from Lower Sandusky.

OFF TO BOARDING SCHOOL

At the time, Rud was not all that interested in going to college or preparing for it. But in June 1836, he went to Norwalk without complaint. (Fanny went to a girls' school in Putnam, Ohio.) Rud did well in his studies, which focused on the classics (writings of ancient Greece and Rome), as well as on public speaking and writing.

In March 1837, at the age of fourteen, Rud decided he was ready for college. (Young people sometimes enrolled in college in their early teens in the 1800s.) His mother felt that Rud was too young for this next step. She was also lonely without her children. So the family decided that Rud would come home to Delaware and continue his studies on his own. This plan did not work out as Sophia had wished. Although Rud was a good student when in school, at home he lost interest in studying. He went sledding in the spring, when there was very little snow, "not so much for the fun," he wrote, "as to say I had slid downhill on the 4th of April." He bragged in a letter to Fanny, who was still away at school, "I have not studied any yet nor shall." He was happy, he wrote, to be "free from the musty crusty fusty rules."

He did not remain free for long. His mother and Uncle Sardis decided that he needed those "musty crusty fusty rules" to buckle down and learn, and that the best place for him to do this was at another boarding school. They chose a school in Connecticut. Despite his loss of freedom, Rud did not lose his good cheer. Happy as he was to loaf around in Delaware, he was also happy to begin a new experience. In October 1837, Rud said good-bye to his mother and headed east to Isaac Webb's Preparatory School in Middletown, Connecticut. His childhood was over. But in many ways, his fun was just beginning.

CHAPTER TWO

STUDENT ON THE MOVE

He is well informed, has good sense, and is respected and esteemed by his companions.
—Schoolmaster Isaac Webb, describing Rutherford B. Hayes, 1837

The Webb School of Middletown, Connecticut, was a small private school, with an enrollment of only twenty boys. The schoolmaster, Isaac Webb, emphasized moral character and discipline as well as academics. The daily schedule left little time for loafing. Wake-up time was 6:30 A.M., with breakfast at 7:00 A.M., followed by prayers. Classes began at 9:00 A.M., with a break at noon for dinner. Then the boys had afternoon classes from 1:00 to 4:00 P.M. After supper, they studied from 6:00 to 9:00 P.M. Saturdays and Sundays the boys had time off.

Rud did not mind the strict schedule. "I like this school very much indeed," he wrote to his Uncle Sardis in December 1837. "All the scholars like the school very much and that is more than can be said of most schools." He made friends quickly.

WORK AND PLAY

Despite the heavy load of class work—nine hours every school day—Rud found time for play. He went ice-skating and played ball. He and his friends took long hikes on Saturday afternoons. His letters revealed a growing sense of humor and love of clever wordplay. He began a letter to his cousin Harriet Moody, "I have forgotten whether I promised to write to you or Sarah or to either of you, but it's no great odds. I am a-going to write to you as you'll begin to suspect by this time." He closed the letter with, "Write right, right off!!!"

Rud did well at the Webb School and earned the head-master's praise. In the spring of 1838, Webb and Uncle Sardis proposed that Rud attend the school for one more year in preparation for attending prestigious Yale College in Connecticut. Rud, however, believed he was already suffi-ciently prepared for college. Also, his mother thought he had spent enough time in the East. She wanted him back in his home state and decided that he should attend Kenyon College in Gambier, Ohio.

Rud agreed with his mother, and their wishes won out. At the end of September 1838, he left Connecticut, head-ing for home. Just after his sixteenth birthday, Rud set foot in Delaware, Ohio, for the first time in a year.

RESISTING RULES

After a month of visiting relatives and friends, hunting, and relaxing, Rud was off to college on November 1, 1838. His

This illustration depicts Kenyon College. The college was founded by an Episcopalian bishop in 1824, with funding from two Englishmen, Lord Kenyon and Lord Gambier.

———————————— ✧ ————————————

classes at Kenyon included logic, Latin, Greek, French, chemistry, biblical literature, natural philosophy (the study of nature), and mathematics. At first, Rud was not sure Kenyon was the place for him. He complained about unchallenging teachers, and he found some of the rules (against cooking in student rooms, for example) unnecessarily strict. In a letter to Fanny in February 1839, he wrote, "Mother wants me to like my teachers. Well, I do like them—a great ways off."

But Rud settled into college life. His classes became more interesting, and he continued to be an excellent student. He also continued to be an outgoing and social young man and made friends with many fellow students.

LOOKING INWARD

Rud's talents for observing and analyzing events and people around him were sharpened at Kenyon by his membership in the Philomathesian Society. This club staged debates and hosted student speeches on a wide variety of topics. Rud was a frequent speaker at Philomathesian events.

He also recorded his observations, including short biographical sketches of his classmates, in a diary. Some entries were comical, others insightful. Of E. T. Austin of Texas, he wrote, "[H]e had no particular traits of character worthy of mention, would do well to trap bullfrogs." Of another Texan friend, Guy Bryan, he wrote, "He is a real gentleman, holds his honor dear, respects the wishes and feelings

✧ ——————————
Hayes formed a lifelong friendship with Texan Guy Bryan.

of others, is a warm and constant friend. . . . He will, I trust, figure largely in Texan history; he is a true patriot."

Rud wrote these biographies in alphabetical order. In the *H* section, he included this one: "R. B. Hayes, Columbus, Ohio.—The owner of this book; remarkable for self-esteem." Rud did have a good opinion of himself, and he knew it. But he also knew he had room for improvement. He was too indecisive, he concluded in the summer of 1841. He vowed, "I am determined from henceforth to . . . acquire a character distinguished for energy, firmness, and perseverance."

At the same time, Rud began thinking seriously about his future. After college, he planned to study law. The choice reflected his excellent debating skills and his desire to earn a good living. "It is another intention of mine," he wrote, "to preserve a reputation for honesty and benevolence [kindness]; and if ever I am a public man I will never do anything inconsistent with the character of a true friend and good citizen."

LEANING TOWARD LEADERSHIP

By the time he was a college senior, Rud had grown into a leader. He was elected president of the Philomathesian Society. Rud studied especially hard during his final year at Kenyon, thinking his efforts would help him become a successful lawyer later.

No matter how seriously he took his studies, though, Rud was never too serious to joke around. He and Fanny kept up a lively correspondence. In January 1842, responding to a letter in which she happened to refer to apples and mince pies, Rud pretended that the very mention of food

Not only was Fanny a good friend and sister to Rud, but she acted as career adviser as well. Fanny wanted Rud to have the sort of prominent career that she could not have. At the time, women did not usually hold jobs at all. This is the only known image of Fanny.

✧ ————————

sent him into a famished frenzy. "But words are too tame to express what then I felt," he wrote back. "A fly in a pot of honey, 'a pig in the clover,' a toad in a gutter,—O pshaw, out with it,—Hayes at the dinner table!"

By this time, Fanny was married and living in Columbus, Ohio. Fanny's first baby, a daughter, died. In the spring of 1842, she gave birth to another girl. Soon afterward, Fanny became seriously ill. She suffered from extreme fatigue and mental illness. Fanny's condition worsened and she became violent. Her psychiatrist and her husband decided to send her to the Ohio Lunatic Asylum, a mental hospital.

When Rud heard news of Fanny's condition, he was extremely upset. His heart was broken for his sister. After some months, Fanny's mental health improved, and she returned home. To Rud's disappointment, she was not well enough to attend his college graduation in August 1842.

Sophia and Uncle Sardis attended, however. They heard Rud deliver two speeches before the students and faculty. The twenty-year-old graduate had grown into a tall and handsome young man. He wore his brown hair parted to one side. His forehead was high, his clean-shaven jaw was square, and his eyes were clear and direct. Rud could not afford fine clothes, but he made a fine appearance anyway. He made his mother and uncle proud.

As for the new graduate, he was, as usual, happy. He also may have felt something like relief. After graduation day was over, he wrote, "I felt of myself all over, and to my astonishment, I found 'twas the same old Rud. Not a single cubit [measurement of length] added to my stature; not a hair's-breadth to my girth. If anything, on the contrary, I felt more lank and gaunt than common, much as if a load were off my stomach."

ON TO HARVARD

After traveling to Michigan to visit a friend, Rud went home to Columbus, Ohio. His mother had moved there from Delaware to live with Fanny, her husband, and their new baby. Their house became Rud's home.

In keeping with his plan to become a lawyer, Rud arranged to study under the supervision of the Columbus law firm of Sparrow and Matthews. (Reading law, as this arrangement was called, was a typical way of becoming a lawyer at the time. Law school was optional.) He also studied German and French on his own, believing that a well-educated person should learn foreign languages.

Rud found this method of learning law to be boring and lonely. He kept at it for almost a year but was happy

*Established in 1636, Harvard has educated several presidents.
Hayes was the third future president to attend the school,
following John Adams and John Quincy Adams.*

———————————————— ✧ ————————————————

when his Uncle Sardis urged him to go to Harvard Law
School instead. In August 1843, Rud traveled east to
Cambridge, Massachusetts, just outside Boston, and
enrolled in the famous law school. Happy to meet up with
several other students from Ohio and a few from the Webb
School, Rud quickly settled back into a school routine.

Besides studying, Rud filled out his time at Harvard by
attending the theater, playing baseball, and visiting New
England relatives. He also attended speeches by famous ora-
tors of the day, such as former president John Quincy
Adams, poet Henry Wadsworth Longfellow, and lawyer and
politician Daniel Webster. He followed the presidential

election of 1844, which pitted Henry Clay of the Whig Party against James Polk of the Democratic Party. Like his Uncle Sardis and many of his friends, Rud backed the Whigs and voted for Clay—his first vote. He was disappointed when Polk carried the election.

Rud's final term at Harvard Law School was coming to a close. On January 1, 1845, he wrote in his diary, "In two or three weeks I shall leave the Law School and soon after shall begin to live. Heretofore I have been getting ready to live. . . . The rudeness of a student must be laid off, and the quiet, manly deportment of a gentleman put on." It was time, in other words, for Rud to be a grown-up.

Hayes's law practice had a slow start, and Hayes quickly became bored and restless. He is pictured here at the age of twenty-four.

CHAPTER THREE

YOUNG LAWYER

Affairs have gone nicely in court and I find myself as tranquil and satisfied as a clam at high tide.

—Rutherford Hayes, reporting on his legal career
to his sister, Fanny, October 23, 1847

Back in Ohio, Hayes settled in Lower Sandusky, the town where his Uncle Sardis lived. He hoped his uncle's contacts might help him attract clients to his legal practice. Hayes formed a law partnership with Ralph Buckland, a friend, and shared a room in a boardinghouse with a cousin.

The law firm of Hayes and Buckland did not exactly take Lower Sandusky by storm. Hayes got some small cases but spent much of his time reading and studying German. As usual, he was optimistic and content. He made fun of the carefree housekeeping in which he and his roommate engaged. In their room, he wrote, "everything like order and neatness is banished from our presence as a nuisance."

TRIP TO TEXAS

Hayes soon longed for a more stimulating career and social life than Lower Sandusky could provide. He decided to move to Cincinnati, in the southwest corner of Ohio on the border with Kentucky. In that larger city, he hoped to build up a more substantial legal practice. Before making this move, Hayes indulged his love of travel. At the invitation of his Kenyon chum Guy Bryan, he and Uncle Sardis journeyed to Texas in December 1848.

When Hayes and his uncle arrived at the Bryan family plantation on the Brazos River, they were treated to Texas-style hospitality. Party guests ate and danced until after four in the morning. As Hayes later wrote in his diary, "These Texans are essentially carnivorous [meat eaters]. Pork ribs, pigs' feet, veal, beef (grand), chickens, venison, and dried meat frequently seen on the table at once."

Along with Texas-style entertainment, Hayes experienced slavery up close during his stay on the plantation. He noted in his diary, "Two little black girls for waiters pass everything possible around, and take the plates of the guests to the carvers, never failing to get the right name." Hayes wrote to his mother that life for a white plantation owner was fashionable and full of pleasures. But slavery was not practiced in Ohio and other northern states, and the notion of slave ownership made Hayes uncomfortable. He added, "I doubt . . . whether a person of Northern education could so far forget his home-bred notions and feelings as ever to be thoroughly Southern on the subject of slavery. . . . I have seen nothing to change my Northern opinions."

TO THE BIG CITY

After two months in Texas, Hayes and his uncle returned to Lower Sandusky. Before moving to Cincinnati, Hayes took on an unusual legal matter. He went to court on behalf of the citizens of Lower Sandusky, who wanted to change the town's name to Fremont. The new name honored John Charles Frémont, known as the Pathfinder for his exploration of western North America.

On Christmas Eve 1849, Hayes left the newly renamed town of Fremont and moved to Cincinnati. His new law practice started off slowly, but he was optimistic as always. By February he had his first case.

In time, Hayes attracted more clients and success. Although he was primarily a business lawyer, his involvement in criminal cases brought him favorable publicity. In one of the most prominent cases, a judge appointed him to help defend Nancy Farrer. The young woman had killed several people by poisoning them. Investigating her background, Hayes realized that she suffered from mental illness. Thinking back to the time when Fanny had been hospitalized for mental illness, Hayes took Farrer's case to heart. He asked each juror in

——————————— ✧

This sketch of Nancy Farrer was drawn in the courtroom at her trial in 1852.

the case to act as though "his own sister or daughter," rather than "this friendless girl," were on trial.

Hayes's arguments did not convince the jury, which found Farrer guilty. But on appeal to the Ohio Supreme Court, Hayes was able to get the guilty verdict overturned. In a new trial, he then succeeded in having Farrer declared insane. She was spared a death sentence and sent instead to a mental institution. Hayes's success in the Nancy Farrer case brought him two other famous murder cases.

"THE GREAT STEP OF LIFE"
While working to build his reputation as a lawyer, Hayes enjoyed an active social life. Most evenings he went to a local gym, where he exercised with friends. Hayes also spent his time reading, attending the theater, and socializing with women.

One of these women was Lucy Ware Webb of Chillicothe, Ohio. Hayes had first met Lucy in 1847, when she was sixteen and attending college. He had seen her on occasion in the years since then. Since he was nine years older than she was, at first Hayes did not think of Lucy as a likely wife. But she was charming, well educated, and attractive, with dark hair, large eyes, and a round, pretty face. By 1851 Lucy was living in Cincinnati with her mother. (Lucy's father had died years earlier.)

Lucy Ware Webb

Hayes and Lucy's wedding portrait
────────────── ✧

Before long, Hayes was in love. He and Lucy married on December 30, 1852. As usual, Hayes poured out his happiness in his diary. "The great step of life which makes or mars the whole after journey, has been happily taken," he wrote. "A better wife I never hoped to have."

To save money, the newlyweds moved in with Lucy's mother in Cincinnati. In November 1853, Lucy gave birth to their first child, a boy named Birchard, or Birch for short. In December that personal milestone was followed by a professional one. Hayes and other Cincinnati attorneys formed the law firm of Corwine, Hayes and Rogers. By the following autumn, with greater prosperity on the horizon, Hayes purchased a house of his own.

BECOMING REPUBLICAN

As Hayes's personal and professional life became more settled, the nation's political life grew more unsettled. The question of slavery was dividing the United States. Within Hayes's Whig Party, people disagreed about whether to allow slavery to continue in the South and in new states being formed out of the western territories.

In his earlier trip to Texas, Hayes had been offended by his observations of slavery in action. In the years since then, he had grown more opposed to slavery. Not only did he feel the practice was morally wrong, but he did not believe that slavery helped the southern economy. Hayes was also influenced by Lucy, who believed slavery should be abolished, or outlawed. Although Hayes did not insist on the abolition of slavery in the South, he opposed the spread of slavery to territories and other states. Many northern Whigs shared Hayes's views. They were infuriated when Congress passed the Kansas-Nebraska Act of 1854. The act allowed the people of Kansas and Nebraska to decide for themselves whether or not to permit slavery when these territories became states.

After the Kansas-Nebraska Act became law, the Whig Party fell apart. Its members took opposing sides on that law and on slavery in general. Many Whigs, including Hayes, joined a new party formed to speak with a clear voice against slavery. This new group called itself the Republican Party.

MOURNING A SISTER

As the nation prepared for a presidential election in 1856, Hayes had other things on his mind. In March of that year, he and Lucy celebrated the birth of their second son, named Webb. Only a few months later, however, their joy was shadowed by sadness. After a difficult pregnancy and the birth of twin girls who died, Hayes's beloved sister, Fanny, died from complications of childbirth.

Hayes was heartsick. "The dearest friend of childhood," he wrote, "the affectionate adviser, the confidante of all my life, the one I loved best is gone, alas!"

Although Hayes would mourn the loss of his sister for the rest of his life, his family life helped cushion the blow. Lucy and his children were very dear to him. He also followed politics with growing interest. Hayes was, in fact, interested in entering public service. But the desire to earn as much money as possible to support his growing family kept him from running for office.

In June 1858, Hayes and Lucy had a third son, named Rutherford (called Ruddy or Rud, as Hayes had been as a boy). The new baby was surely one more reason for Hayes to stick to the moneymaking practice of law. But soon Hayes was offered a high-paying public service job. In December 1858, the Cincinnati City Council selected him to replace the city solicitor (law officer), who had recently died. This was an exciting post. The city solicitor handled all the interesting lawsuits involving the city and also provided legal advice to city officials.

Hayes did a good job as city solicitor, and in April 1859 he was reelected by a popular vote (a vote of the city's male citizens). The position—and his continuing involvement in the Ohio Republican Party—gave Hayes prominence in Cincinnati and throughout Ohio.

NATION IN TURMOIL
The following year, 1860, Abraham Lincoln became the Republican candidate for president. He ran against three other candidates. Lincoln ran on a promise to halt the

spread of slavery into new states. He would take no action against slavery in states where it already existed.

Hayes enthusiastically backed Lincoln. Not all Americans shared Hayes's enthusiasm, however. Some southern states, led by South Carolina, threatened to secede, or leave the Union (United States), if Lincoln won the election.

Abraham Lincoln did win the election. With his victory, the nation moved into crisis. In late December 1860, the South Carolina legislature voted to secede from the Union, declaring the laws of the United States invalid in that state. More southern states followed, for a total of eleven.

——————————— ◇ ———————————

This Republican campaign poster for the 1860 election features Abraham Lincoln and his running mate, Hannibal Hamlin.

Of the seceding states, Hayes wrote in his diary, "Let them go." He believed the country could and should continue as a "glorious nation" of free states. There would be a war, he thought. But it would be a brief conflict, with the limited goal of creating clear boundaries between the free nation and the slave states that chose to leave.

In February 1861, the seceding states formed a government called the Confederate States of America, also called the Confederacy. Lincoln took his oath of office as the sixteenth president of the United States on March 4, 1861.

A few weeks later, in local elections in Cincinnati, the Republicans took a beating. The city's Democratic voters, many of whom felt a bond toward the South, ousted Hayes and other Republicans from office. Although Cincinnati was part of a northern state, it shared a border with the slave state of Kentucky. Many Cincinnatians were sympathetic to the southern cause.

Hayes had anticipated his defeat and took it in stride. He set up a new law firm in partnership with Leopold Markbreit, who came from a well-connected German American family. Hayes hoped the firm would attract clients from Cincinnati's large German American community.

Perhaps the law firm of Hayes and Markbreit would have had great success, but it never had a chance to do business. At 4:30 A.M. on April 12, 1861, South Carolina troops attacked Union troops stationed at Fort Sumter in the harbor of Charleston, South Carolina. The Civil War (1861–1865) had begun, and Rutherford B. Hayes was not going to spend it in a courtroom.

Nearly forty when the Civil War started, Hayes was one of the first to volunteer as a soldier. He was quickly promoted to colonel, then brigadier general.

CHAPTER FOUR

UNION SOLDIER

*I would prefer to go into it [the Civil War] if
I knew I was to die or be killed in the course
of it, than to live through and after it without
taking any part in it.*
—Rutherford B. Hayes, diary entry, May 15, 1861

Hayes's ideas about the Civil War changed after the attack
on Fort Sumter. His "let them go" attitude toward the
seceding states faded when President Lincoln asked northern states to provide seventy-five thousand soldiers to fight
to keep the South in the Union. In May 1861, Hayes
signed up for army service. The nation was moving into "a
just and necessary war," he wrote in his diary, that "demand-
ed the whole power of the country"—including him.

OFF TO WAR
Hayes joined the Twenty-third Ohio Regiment, which was
then camped at a racetrack outside Columbus, Ohio. The

governor of Ohio made Hayes an officer, with the rank of major. Hayes was responsible for the enlisted men of the Twenty-third.

Military life suited Hayes. A few days after meeting his regiment, Hayes wrote to his Uncle Sardis, "I enjoy this thing very much. It is open-air, active life, novel and romantic." Explaining that he and his friend Stanley Matthews were in charge of the camp's daily routine, he wrote, "What we don't know, we guess at, and you may be sure we are kept pretty busy guessing."

At the end of July 1861, the Twenty-third moved into the northwestern region of Virginia, a Confederate state bordering Ohio. (Later in the war, the northwestern counties of Virginia, which wanted to remain in the Union, formed a new state, West Virginia.) At first, the soldiers encountered no Confederates, only loyal Unionists. "It was pleasant to see we were not invading an enemy's country but defending the people among whom we came," Hayes wrote to Lucy.

TASTING BATTLE

The feeling of being among friends did not last. On September 10, 1861, Hayes saw battle for the first time. He led four companies of the Twenty-third to fight Confederate forces in the hills of Carnifex Ferry in western Virginia. The Union soldiers forced the Confederates to retreat across the Gauley River. Of his first experience in battle, Hayes wrote in his diary, "My feelings were not different from what I have often felt before beginning an important lawsuit. As we waited for our turn to form [into ranks], we joked a great deal."

After this encounter, in the fall of 1861, Hayes was ordered out of combat to serve as a judge advocate, or military lawyer. The assignment entitled him to privileges, such as a clerk to help him with paperwork and an aide to assist with other tasks. But he was not happy to be separated from his regiment. He did not have to suffer for long, however. At the end of October 1861, he was promoted to the rank of lieutenant colonel and reunited with the Twenty-third as a fighting soldier.

Shortly after he rejoined the Twenty-third, Hayes and his regiment set up their winter camp in Fayetteville, Virginia, southwest of Carnifex Ferry. During the winter, runaway slaves made their way to the Union soldiers' encampment to obtain freedom. In January 1862, Hayes noted in his diary, "These runaways . . . are superior to the average of the uneducated white population of this State. More intelligent, I feel

─────────────────── ✧ ───────────────────

Runaway slaves gather in Virginia in 1862. Many male runaways fought in the Civil War alongside Union soldiers.

confident." By this time, Hayes no longer felt the war should merely establish boundaries between slave and free states. He wanted slavery outlawed, even in the South.

After Lucy gave birth to their fourth son, named Joseph, Hayes went home for a visit in February 1862. He showed off his full beard, the result of months of not shaving. The family had a joyful reunion.

RETREAT AT PEARISBURG

In the spring, Hayes and his regiment were back in action. Heading south, Hayes and his men drove Confederates out of the town of Princeton, Virginia. Hayes was extremely proud of the Twenty-third's victory and his men's bravery. "Sergeant Ritter had a bullet shot into his head lodging between the scalp and skull," Hayes wrote. "He fell, but instantly jumped up saying, 'You must shoot lower if you want to kill me.'"

Hayes and his men pressed farther southeast into Pearisburg, Virginia. Confederate forces opened fire on the Twenty-third, which had to make a difficult retreat. Hayes's knee was slightly injured by a piece of shell. In a letter to Lucy, he described the retreat as "well-ordered," but he may have been more shaken than he admitted. In a diary entry dated "Sunday (?) May 11," he wrote: "This is the first Sunday that has passed without my knowing the day of the week since childhood."

BATTLE OF SOUTH MOUNTAIN

In August 1862, the Twenty-third received orders to head east to join the Union Army of Virginia. (The army would soon be called the Grand Army of the Potomac.) The troops made their way east by foot, steamboat, and railroad. On September 14, Union forces, including Hayes and his regiment, were sent to fight Confederate soldiers holding South Mountain in Maryland. South Mountain was a ridge between the town of Frederick to the east and Sharpsburg to the west.

Hayes's superiors ordered the Twenty-third out in front of a dangerous uphill assault on Confederate positions. With Confederate fire raining down, Hayes ordered his men to make a series of charges. As he did so, Hayes felt what he described as "a stunning blow." A musket ball struck his left arm above the elbow. Bleeding and feeling sick, he lay down in the woods as fighting continued all around.

———————————— ✧ ————————————

During the Battle of South Mountain (below), Hayes led his men in an attack against Confederate troops at a place called Fox's Gap. There, he received his second wound of the war.

Because of blood loss, Hayes was weak and also possibly drifting in and out of consciousness. Separated from his men, he was no longer in a position to lead them. Hayes had company out there in the no-man's-land between the two armies. "While I was lying down I had considerable talk with a wounded [Confederate] soldier lying near me," Hayes later wrote in his diary. "I gave him messages for my wife and friends in case I should not get up. We were right jolly and friendly; it was by no means an unpleasant experience."

After the fighting quieted down, Hayes's men moved him out of danger. In nearby Middletown, Maryland, a Union-friendly family took him in. Hayes showed his good cheer when he wrote to his mother, "I am comfortably at home with a very kind and attentive family here named Rudy—not quite Ruddy."

SIDELINED BY INJURY

The Battle of South Mountain was a victory for the Union. With the ridge clear, the Union army pushed west to meet the Confederates in Sharpsburg, Maryland, at a small stream called Antietam Creek. In the bloody Battle of Antietam, on September 17, 1862, the Union army stopped the Confederate advance into the North, at least for the time being.

Hayes's wound was painful and slow to heal. He celebrated his fortieth birthday while recuperating in the Rudy home. When they received news of his injury, his Uncle Sardis, friends, and acquaintances urged him to quit the army. They felt that he had sufficiently served his country on the battlefield. If he wished to serve further, they suggested, he should run for Congress.

THE LIGHTER SIDE

From boyhood, Rutherford Hayes was a person who liked a laugh. When he was young, teasing his sister, Fanny, was the hallmark of his humor. In a letter to Fanny from Kenyon College, Hayes wrote, "I am astonished at your cruelty in preferring quills [large feathers, the sharp ends of which are dipped in ink and used as pens] to steel pens, for in using a steel pen you are assisting thousands of poor souls to gain their bread, [including] ironmongers, miners, blacksmiths, etc. . . . but on the other hand you would reflect upon the pain of Madame Goose and Mr. Gander in having their feathers plucked out by the roots. Oh! it is horrid to think on, tho I am now using quills myself."

Later, when he was a parent, Hayes enjoyed telling amusing stories in which his children were the star attractions. In November 1857, he recorded this tale about his eldest son, Birch:

> He asked his mother who the preacher talked to when he shut his eyes and looked up. She replied, "to God." "But where is God?"—"In Heaven where good people are after they are dead."—"How do good people get up there?"—"God takes them."—"How do God take them up?" His mother hesitated. "Do He pull them up with a rope?"

Even when he was recovering from the serious injury he received at the Battle of South Mountain, Hayes tried to amuse his mother with this story from his sickbed: "A little boy . . . named Charlie Rudy, sits by the window and describes the troops, etc., etc., as they pass. I said to him, 'Charlie, you live on a street that is much travelled.' 'Oh,' said he, 'it isn't always so, it's only when the war comes.'"

But Hayes wanted to remain in the army. In late October, he received a promotion to the rank of full colonel in command of the Twenty-third Regiment. After a long visit home in Ohio to recuperate further, Hayes returned to his regiment late in November 1862.

BACK TO WEST VIRGINIA

Hayes's regiment went into winter camp in West Virginia, which was then in the process of achieving statehood. While in camp, Hayes kept up with the national news. He cheered President Lincoln's Emancipation Proclamation of January 1, 1863, which freed all slaves living in the Confederacy. His greatest diversion that winter came when Lucy and their two oldest boys, Birch and Webb, joined him at the end of January for a two-month visit. Neither snow nor rain nor mud stopped them from enjoying rowing and fishing on the Kanawha River.

In March Hayes and his men moved to a new headquarters farther down the Kanawha River near Charleston, West Virginia. (By then he led several other regiments and companies in addition to the Twenty-third.) The situation was so calm that in June, Hayes invited Lucy and all four boys, as well as Lucy's mother, for another visit. Their happy visit soon turned sad when Joe, who was then eighteen months old, suddenly became sick and died. Hayes had barely known his youngest son.

"A CRUEL BUSINESS"

The Hayeses' sad personal loss was soon followed by encouraging war news. Union soldiers won the Battle of Gettysburg in Pennsylvania in early July 1863, and the

The Battle of Gettysburg in 1863 is often considered the turning point of the Civil War. More men died in this battle on U.S. soil than in any other battle before or since.

———————— ✧ ————————

Mississippi town of Vicksburg surrendered to the Union army on July 4 after a forty-eight-day siege. The fighting at Gettysburg had resulted in staggering numbers of dead and wounded. Still, the victory there and at Vicksburg was cheering news to Hayes and other northerners.

The spring of 1864 began a season of renewed fighting for Hayes. He and his men carried out a campaign led by General George Crook to destroy railroad lines in Virginia. This was part of a Union strategy to cut off Confederate supply lines. Hayes and his brigade joined up with General David Hunter's army and captured Lexington, Virginia.

But Hayes lost respect for Hunter when the general ordered soldiers to burn the Virginia Military Institute and the home of the Virginia governor. Hayes was coura-geous and fiercely loyal to the Union cause, but he despised such needless destruction and cruelty. He described the burning of the revered Virginia institutions as "surely bad." He also recognized that both armies had their share of wrongdoers. "War is a cruel business," he wrote to Lucy in July 1864, "and there is brutality in it on all sides."

ABSENT CANDIDATE

In mid-July, General Crook's army of twelve thousand soldiers, including Hayes's men, endured a defeat at Confederate hands in Winchester, Virginia. Hayes received his third wound of the war when he was shot in the shoulder there.

While Hayes was living the life of a soldier in Virginia, friends back in Ohio were planning a different future for him—as a politician. They nominated him as the Republican candidate for the U.S. House of Representatives, representing the Cincinnati district. Hayes agreed to stand as a candidate, but he refused to campaign. When a supporter urged him to take a leave from the army to come home and campaign, Hayes declined even more strongly. "An officer fit for duty who at this crisis would abandon his post to electioneer for a seat in Congress ought to be scalped," he wrote back.

DIFFERENT SORT OF VICTORY

The new congressional candidate turned his attention back to the battlefield. In autumn 1864, Hayes and his men repeatedly fought the Confederates in Virginia's Shenandoah

Valley. These were difficult battles. In one of the fights, at
the Battle of Cedar Creek, Hayes's horse was shot out from
under him. Hayes took a bad fall and injured his foot and
ankle. But he escaped serious injury, and the Union army
pulled out an important victory. For his role in the
Shenandoah Valley battles, Hayes received a promotion to
the rank of brigadier general.

Meanwhile, Hayes had a different sort of victory back
in Ohio. Thanks to the efforts of friends and supporters,
he won election to the U.S. House of Representatives in
October 1864. However, he had not personally campaigned a single day. (His term of office was not to
begin for more than a year, in late 1865.) He had another reason to celebrate when Lucy gave birth to their fifth
son, George Crook Hayes. They named the child after
Hayes's commanding offi-
cer, whom he liked so well.

✧ ————————————

*General George Crook (left) was
Hayes's commanding officer. After
the Civil War, General Crook fought
Native Americans in the West.*

CONFEDERATE SURRENDER

The war was winding down. In March 1865, Hayes received further recognition for his achievements in battle when he was made a major general. Before he could enter battle again, however, Confederate general Robert E. Lee surrendered his army to Union general Ulysses S. Grant at Appomattox Courthouse, Virginia. The date was April 9, 1865. The Civil War was over.

———————————— ◇ ————————————

General Lee (right) surrenders to General Grant (left) in 1865, bringing an end to the Civil War.

Hayes was jubilant. His happiness turned to despair days later. On April 14, assassin John Wilkes Booth murdered President Lincoln while the president was attending a play at Ford's Theatre in Washington, D.C. Hayes reflected on the president's life in a letter: "His firmness, moderation, goodness of heart; his quaint humor, his perfect honesty and directness of purpose . . . elevate him to a place in history second to none other of ancient or modern times."

Millions of people, mostly in the North, shared Hayes's opinion. Others, mostly in the South, did not. The two sides would no longer be fighting out their differences on the battlefield. Their disputes moved to Congress, which needed to decide the future of the South, of the former slaves, and of the reunited country. And Rutherford Hayes was moving to Congress as well.

As a U.S. congressman, Hayes attended sessions regularly. He spoke little and supported measures to rebuild the South.

CHAPTER FIVE

CONGRESSMAN AND GOVERNOR

They [African Americans] are not aliens or strangers. . . . They are here by the misfortune of their fathers and the crime of ours. Their labor . . . and sufferings . . . have cleared and redeemed one third of the inhabited territory of the Union. . . . Whether we prefer it or not, they are our countrymen, and will remain so forever.
—Rutherford Hayes, urging Ohioans to accept voting rights for black Americans, 1867

Congressman Hayes started his new career in Washington, D.C., on November 30, 1865. Lucy and the four boys remained in Cincinnati. The new congressman moved into the first floor of a boardinghouse. His accommodations consisted of a front room, a parlor, and a back room.

Once settled, Hayes attended meetings with other Republicans to create strategies for the upcoming congressional session. The Republicans had a majority in Congress. They were eager to counter actions taken by President Andrew Johnson earlier in the year, when Congress had not been assembled.

Congressional Republicans believed that the governments of the southern states needed to be "reconstructed," or rebuilt from scratch, with Republicans in charge. In contrast, Johnson wanted simply to restore the South to the Union without requiring much in the way of political change. During the congressional recess (break), Johnson had announced that southern states could reestablish their governments. They would have elections held by citizens who had been qualified to vote in 1860. He did not require the southern states to ensure rights for the newly freed former slaves.

As a result, white southerners had created "new" state governments. They were full of former Confederate leaders whose ideas about the rights and freedoms of black Americans had not changed since slavery days. Southern legislatures (lawmakers) quickly passed "black codes." These laws deprived black people of any voice in their government and any meaningful rights. For example, the codes required most black people to work on farms, toiling long hours in the fields for minimal pay. To do any other type of work, a black person had to gain special permission from a white official, such as a judge. Black citizens were prohibited from freely moving about in towns or the countryside. They could not serve on juries, vote, hold office, or marry white people. Southern states also elected former Confederate leaders to serve in Congress.

In their meetings, congressional Republicans agreed that southern representatives should not be permitted to take seats in Congress without further investigation. They also pronounced the new southern state governments illegal. When the Thirty-ninth Congress formally met on December 4, 1865, it easily adopted these guidelines. A strong Republican, Hayes endorsed these actions.

VOTING FOR CIVIL RIGHTS

President Johnson refused to embrace Congress's Reconstruction policies. Congress passed the Civil Rights Act. The act guaranteed black Americans rights as citizens and equal protection, or equal treatment, under the laws. Johnson vetoed, or blocked, the act in March 1866. Hayes had hoped the president and Congress might work together, but he gave up that hope. He voted with other Republicans to override (reject) Johnson's veto. The Civil Rights Act became law in April 1866, despite the president's disagreement.

Johnson's refusal to cooperate with Congress—and the continued oppression of blacks in the South—moved Hayes to support the proposed Fourteenth Amendment to the U.S. Constitution. The Thirteenth Amendment, adopted in 1865, had outlawed slavery. Yet southern governments were still treating black Americans as less than citizens. Under the proposed Fourteenth Amendment, no state could deny equal protection of the laws to people within its borders.

Congress passed the Fourteenth Amendment. Then, following the rules for amending the Constitution, Congress sent it to the states for their approval. President Johnson urged states not to adopt the amendment. Except for Tennessee, the southern states all rejected the amendment.

FRANK LESLIE'S ILLUSTRATED NEWSPAPER.

MENDING THE FAMILY KETTLE.

COLUMBIA—" Now, Andy, I wish you and your boys would hurry up that job, because I want to hat kettle right away. You are all talking too much about it."

This cartoon criticizes the Johnson administration for not acting swiftly on Reconstruction measures. The woman on the left, representing liberty, holds a baby representing the Fourteenth Amendment (equal protection under the law). The woman wants Johnson (right) to fix the South, represented by the leaky teakettle he is holding.

✧ ————————

RECONSTRUCTION BEGINS

While Congress clashed with the president, Hayes was distracted by several sad personal losses. In May 1866, his youngest son, George, died of scarlet fever. George had been born while Hayes was in Virginia fighting the Civil War. He died while Hayes was in Washington, D.C., engaged in the fight over the future of the South. Then in the fall, Lucy's mother died, followed by the death of Hayes's mother.

Hayes mourned his losses but carried on with his work. He won reelection to Congress in the 1866 autumn elections. Republicans had no hope of southern states voluntarily adopting the Fourteenth Amendment. So they came up with a Reconstruction plan that was much stricter than before. It was known as radical Reconstruction.

Under the new Reconstruction Act, southern states would be placed under federal, or U.S. government, control. (The act did not apply to Tennessee, which had accepted the Fourteenth Amendment.) Federal troops would enforce the rights of the states' black citizens. Once a southern state guaranteed black men the right to vote and approved the Fourteenth Amendment, its representatives would be seated in Congress. (In those days, all women were denied voting rights.) Federal troops would leave the state.

Hayes voted for the Reconstruction Act. President Johnson vetoed the bill on March 2, 1867, but Congress overrode his veto that same day. The era of Reconstruction had begun.

——————— ✧

This political cartoon shows southerners opposing Reconstruction. The text at the bottom reflects the Democratic belief that the Reconstruction Acts were unconstitutional.

CAMPAIGN FOR GOVERNOR

As Reconstruction began, Hayes's congressional career came to an end. Friends back in Ohio urged him to run for governor in the autumn 1867 election. The idea appealed to Hayes. Ohio Republicans nominated him as their candidate for the governorship in June 1867. At the conclusion of the congressional session in July, Hayes resigned his seat in the House of Representatives and went home to campaign. The main issue in the election was familiar to him: political rights for African Americans.

In his speeches, Hayes argued that Ohio should adopt a state constitutional amendment guaranteeing the vote to its black male citizens. His Democratic opponent argued against the amendment. This position was popular with many voters in the state.

The campaign ended as Hayes celebrated his forty-fifth birthday on October 4, 1867. With many Democratic voters in the state, he was sure he would lose. Even so, he was cheerful. He and Lucy had a new baby girl, Fanny, born in the middle of the campaign. Hayes was happy to be back in Ohio with his family. "Now for a sensible future," he wrote to Uncle Sardis before the votes had been counted.

In the end, Hayes won the election by a narrow margin of votes. But Hayes and the Republicans lost the heart of the election. Voters defeated the constitutional amendment giving black men the right to vote. Voters also elected a majority of Democrats to the state legislature. With Hayes's victory, Ohio Republicans had won a battle of sorts. But Democrats had captured the larger prize.

THE "PLEASANTEST" JOB

Hayes took over the governorship on January 13, 1868, with energy and interest. He, Lucy, baby Fanny, and young Rud moved to Columbus, Ohio, the state capital. Sons Birch and Webb, then in their teens, lived and studied with Uncle Sardis in Fremont.

The governorship did not carry much power. Under the Ohio constitution, the governor could not veto acts of the legislature. This limited Hayes's ability to shape state policies. This restriction

Hayes as governor in the 1860s
——————— ✧ ———————

did not lessen Hayes's enjoyment of his new job. "It strikes me . . . as the pleasantest I have ever had," he wrote to Uncle Sardis early in his term. "Not too much hard work, plenty of time to read, good society, etc."

Hayes exercised the few powers he did have with care. He appointed state judges and members of various boards of directors that ran state colleges and charities. He granted or denied pardons to people who had been convicted of crimes. He decided to send young people who had committed crimes to reform school, rather than have them mix with hardened criminals in prison.

Hayes also stayed active in national politics. He was pleased when the Fourteenth Amendment finally became

A popular war general, Ulysses S. Grant (left) easily won the 1868 presidential election even though he barely campaigned.

✧ ——————————

part of the Constitution in 1868. In the presidential election of 1868, he campaigned for the Republican candidate, former Civil War general Ulysses S. Grant. Grant won the election to become the eighteenth president.

ON A ROLL

Hayes was up for reelection in 1869. The Democratic legislature of Ohio had recently rejected the proposed Fifteenth Amendment to the U.S. Constitution. This amendment declared that the right to vote "shall not be denied or abridged by the United States or by any State on account of race, color, or previous condition of servitude." The legislature had also passed a law that denied voting rights to men of mixed race. In his campaign, Hayes slammed the Democrats for their racism.

Hayes was popular with voters, and his record in the Civil War appealed to many. Not only did he win the election, Ohio Republicans also won back a slender majority in the state legislature that year.

With Republicans in the legislature, Hayes was able to carry out some of his ideas. Responding to Hayes's requests, the legislature repealed the law that deprived the vote to men of mixed race. The legislature also funded the Ohio Agricultural and Mechanical College (which later became Ohio State University). The lawmakers agreed to improve state facilities for orphans and the mentally ill. The legislature also passed the Fifteenth Amendment.

During his second term, Hayes indulged his love of travel. He visited Washington, D.C., in the summer of 1870. This trip was followed by trips to reunions of Civil War soldiers and visits to Wisconsin and Minnesota. In the fall of 1870, he traveled to Ithaca, New York, where he enrolled his son Birch in Cornell University. Another son, named Scott, was born in February 1871. After his birth, Hayes traveled to Virginia's Shenandoah Valley, Kenyon College, Vermont, Connecticut, and New York. On some of these trips, he took care of state business, but he also enjoyed sightseeing and visiting friends during his travels.

Although Hayes enjoyed his terms as governor, he felt ready to leave politics. He believed that the main challenges facing the nation—the abolition of slavery and Reconstruction—were settled. He decided not to seek a third term as governor.

PUSHED TO RUN

Hayes retired as governor on January 8, 1872. "I am a free man again," he wrote to a friend, "and jolly as a beggar." He turned to financial pursuits such as investing money in land and railroads. Hayes and Lucy intended to make Fremont, Ohio, their permanent home. Aging Uncle Sardis

Spiegel Grove, the home Sardis Birchard left to Hayes, was originally an eight-bedroom estate. Through the years, Hayes added many additions, turning the home into a thirty-one-room mansion.

———————————————— ✧ ————————————————

had decided to give them his estate there, called Spiegel Grove. For the time being, however, Hayes, Lucy, Fanny, and little Scott moved to Cincinnati. By then, Birch, Webb, and Rud were all away at school.

Although he enjoyed his new line of work, Hayes let himself be drafted back into politics in the summer of 1872. President Grant was the Republican Party's nominee for the upcoming presidential election. But he had lost the support of many Republicans. So-called liberal Republicans objected to Grant, especially his administration's reputation for corruption (misdeeds such as taking bribes). Pro-Grant Republicans begged Hayes to run for Congress again, if only to help President Grant win reelection. They argued that if Hayes was a candidate, Republicans who supported him would line up behind Grant as well. Hayes went along with the nomination and threw himself into a new campaign.

Hayes ran on his usual issue of supporting political rights for blacks. Despite his support for President Grant, Hayes also addressed the problem of corruption in the Grant administration. He wanted the government to reform civil service laws—rules about the hiring and official conduct of government employees. Hayes and others wanted to make sure the government was staffed with honest public servants who obtained their jobs fairly and who did not take bribes from people seeking special treatment from the government.

When the ballots were counted in the October congressional election, Hayes lost to his Democratic opponent. But he was happy not to be going back to Washington, D.C. He was even happier at the outcome of the November balloting for president. President Grant won by a large margin and carried the state of Ohio.

FAMILY FIRST

Hayes embraced private life with renewed energy. In 1873 the family moved to Spiegel Grove. There, Hayes set to work enlarging the house that Uncle Sardis had given him. In August 1873, Lucy gave birth to their eighth child, a boy named Manning.

That same year, the nation suffered a severe economic depression, called the Panic of 1873. Banks and businesses failed, and stock prices plummeted. Millions of people were thrown out of work. Hayes's business interests did poorly, but he and his family did not suffer. When Uncle Sardis died in January 1874, Hayes settled his uncle's business affairs. Sadly, the youngest Hayes child, Manning, died just after his first birthday in the summer of 1874.

Even with a business slump and the loss of a child, Hayes did not lose pleasure in his family life. One Thursday in mid-March 1875, he wrote in his diary, "We put Fanny and Scott each on a sled with an umbrella on the pond where the ice is clear and smooth. The wind drove them along pleasantly. . . . Birch and I enjoyed it quite as much as the children."

———————————— ✧ ————————————

Hayes greatly enjoyed time with his family. Seated (from left to right) *are Hayes, Scott, daughter Fanny, and Lucy. Standing in the back row* (from left to right) *are Webb, Birchard, and Rutherford.*

BACK INTO THE FRAY

While Hayes immersed himself in his private and family life, the nation's political life was again in turmoil. Northern voters were unhappy with the Republicans' handling of the economic crisis and with corruption in the Grant administration. They had turned once again to the Democratic Party. The Democrats had won back the governorship and legislature in Ohio. In the South, Democrats engaged in violence and intimidation to keep black men— who generally voted Republican—from going to the polls during elections. In the 1874 elections, voters elected a Democratic majority to the U.S. House of Representatives for the first time since before the Civil War.

Once again, Hayes was drawn into the struggle. He was a proven vote-getter, and the Republican Party needed him. Ohio Republicans convinced him to run for a third term as governor in the fall of 1875. Hayes made speeches every day throughout the month of September. His efforts paid off. When the Ohio polls closed in the election of October 1875, Hayes had won a third term as governor. Republicans had also won back the state legislature.

As hero of the Republican Party of Ohio, Hayes immediately was crowned the potential hero of Republicans nationwide. As soon as the election results were announced, ten Ohio newspapers backed Hayes for president in the 1876 election. Others in and out of Ohio took up the call.

Meanwhile, Hayes moved from Spiegel Grove to Columbus to take up his duties as governor. The office, he wrote, was so familiar that it was "like getting into old slippers."

LIBERTY AND UNION

GOV. RUTHERFORD B. HAYES,

HON. WM. A. WHEELER

FOR PRESIDENT.

FOR VICE-PRESIDENT.

GRAND NATIONAL REPUBLICAN BANNER.

The Republican campaign banner for the 1876 presidential election was designed by a printing company called Currier & Ives. The company produced a similar banner for the Democratic ticket that same year.

CHAPTER SIX

ELECTION OF 1876

*I have no doubt that we are justly and legally
entitled to the Presidency.*

—Rutherford Hayes, during the 1876 election
controversy

On June 14, 1876, delegates assembled at the Republican
National Convention in Cincinnati to choose their candidate
for president in the upcoming election. For the first time
since 1860, the party's presidential nomination was hotly
contested. Six men, including Rutherford Hayes, hoped to
be chosen as the Republicans' candidate for president.

The six men did not attend the convention or openly
campaign among other Republicans. Candidates for president
in those days left that kind of work to their supporters. Still,
Hayes and the others campaigned behind the scenes.
Although he was well liked, Hayes was not the leader of the
pack. That honor belonged to Congressman James Blaine of
Maine, Speaker of the House of Representatives.

After supporters for the candidates made speeches at the convention, the balloting began on June 16. On the first vote, Blaine was the leader by a large margin. Hayes trailed fifth out of the six candidates. Despite his lead, Blaine had not obtained the majority needed to clinch the nomination. So the convention had to take a second ballot and then a third and a fourth.

After the fourth ballot, convention delegates began to shift their support to Hayes. His appeal was considerable. As a Civil War hero, he would attract many patriotic northern voters. As an Ohio man, he would nearly ensure that Republicans would win that important state in the fall. And Hayes's reputation for honesty and fair dealing was untarnished.

On the fifth ballot, Hayes took the lead, although not a majority. He became the Republican nominee for president on the seventh ballot, late in the afternoon. The convention then voted William Wheeler, a congressman from New York, as its nominee for vice president.

HEATED CAMPAIGN

The Democratic Party also chose a governor—New York governor Samuel J. Tilden—as its presidential candidate in 1876. Like Hayes, Tilden enjoyed a reputation for clean government. He had helped put an end to corrupt government practices in his state. Thomas Hendricks of Indiana was Tilden's vice-presidential running mate.

As was the custom of the era, neither of the presidential candidates traveled the country stumping for votes. Instead, the candidates issued formal letters setting forth their positions on various issues. They let others do the campaigning.

Tilden (right), the Democratic candidate for president in 1876, proved a tough opponent for Hayes. Tilden had excellent reform credentials. He had successfully fought dishonest government practices in New York while he was governor of the state.
──────────────── ✧

In his letter, Hayes promised reform of the civil service. He called for the protection of the rights of African Americans. Hayes also announced that if elected, he would serve only one term. This promise meant that no one could accuse him of handing out jobs or political favors in exchange for support for a second term. Beyond these statements, he remained in the background of the campaign.

It was a heated campaign. Some Republicans tried to stay on a positive theme by emphasizing Hayes's desire for true government reform. But the Democrats had the upper hand on that issue, as Tilden was famous for fighting corruption in New York. The Democrats also had the advantage of being the party out of power. They could blame everything that was wrong with the country on the Republicans.

In response, many Republicans dropped the positive, forward-looking theme of reform. They went for a more

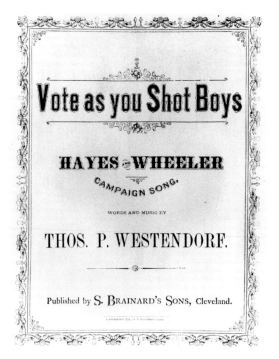

Many nineteenth-century political campaigns relied on songs to spread the word about candidates. This is the cover of a piece of sheet music created for the 1876 Hayes campaign.
✧ ————————

emotional reaction. "Vote as you shot," they urged northerners. The Civil War had been over for only a decade. Republican strategists knew they could stir up votes for their candidate by reminding northerners that the Democratic Party was the party of the Confederacy.

Hayes himself favored this approach. As he wrote to a supporter on October 5, 1876, "The people do dread a victory for the united South. They see in it continued trouble; nullification of [an end to] the Amendments, Rebel [Confederate] claims, and schemes . . . and I think anything which withdraws attention from this issue . . . is a mistake."

As Hayes wrote, the South was indeed in "continued trouble." Reconstruction had not worked. Florida, Louisiana, and South Carolina still had Republican Reconstruction governments, protected by federal troops. The other eight states of the former Confederacy had gone through the motions necessary to get rid of federal rule and reestablish their own governments. They had adopted the Fourteenth and Fifteenth amendments. However, both were dead letters—laws that were ignored. With the help of racist terror groups, white Democrats in the eight states trampled black rights and set up white-only rule. Bands of white supremacists (those who argued for the superiority of the white race) assaulted and even murdered black citizens. They used violence against blacks who dared to attempt to vote.

───────────────── ❖ ─────────────────

One white supremacy group that formed after the Civil War was the Ku Klux Klan (KKK). This etching shows how some members of the KKK disguised themselves in the late 1800s.

DISPUTED ELECTION

Election day fell on November 7, 1876. Early reports of the results were not encouraging. Although Hayes made a strong showing in the North, Tilden seemed to have captured enough states to carry the whole country. In some ways, Hayes was relieved. He and Lucy talked about what a pleasant life they would have without the burdens of the U.S. presidency.

But as night turned into day on November 8, it became clear that the race was still on. The outcome hinged on South Carolina, Louisiana, and Florida. In these three states—the southern states that still had Reconstruction governments—the Republicans still had a chance. If Tilden won any one of these states, he would have enough votes to win the election. Hayes needed to win all three to overcome Tilden's lead. But the outcomes were in dispute. When Republicans counted the votes in the three states, they pronounced Hayes the winner. When Democrats added up the ballots, Tilden won.

Five days after the election, the debate still raged. Hayes was convinced that southern Democrats had cheated at the ballot box. He thought they had tampered with votes and used violence and intimidation to prevent black Republicans from voting. Later in the month, the dispute was still dragging on. Hayes told a friend that he did not want his fellow Republicans also tinkering with votes in illegal ways. "There must be nothing crooked on our part. Let Mr. Tilden have the place [the presidency] by violence, intimidation, and fraud, rather than undertake to prevent it by means that will not bear the severest scrutiny."

But Republican Party activists were not willing to accept defeat so philosophically. They insisted that their tallies

This cartoon appeared in a New York City newspaper in January 1877, while the results of the 1876 election were still undecided. It shows a soldier thrusting the contested election returns from South Carolina, Louisiana, and Florida at Hayes.

——————————————— ✧ ———————————————

(vote counts), not the Democrats', were correct. Days turned into weeks as Democrats and Republicans argued. The deadline for the states to submit their final results to Congress was in early December. South Carolina, Louisiana, and Florida sent in two sets of results, one from Republicans and the other by Democrats.

The argument and delay continued as Congress debated which election results to accept. The writers of the Constitution had not anticipated such a problem, and the document did not provide the answer. Finally, in January 1877, Congress set up a special Electoral Commission to weigh the conflicting tallies. The commission had fifteen members—five senators, five representatives, and five Supreme

Court justices. Seven of the members were Democrats, seven were Republicans, and one, Supreme Court justice David Davis, was not connected to either political party.

At the last minute, Davis had to withdraw from the commission when he unexpectedly won election to the Senate. Under the rules governing the commission, Davis's replacement had to be drawn from the Supreme Court. The remaining Supreme Court justices were all Republicans. So the commission ended up with an eight-to-seven Republican majority.

On February 1, 1877, Congress began its official count. When the count reached the disputed states, proceedings stopped so that the fifteen-member Electoral Commission could hear arguments from both sides. In each case, the commission voted eight-to-seven to award the state to Hayes. The eight Republicans voted for the Republican count, and the seven Democrats backed the Democratic tally.

The presidency seemed to belong to Hayes. He shifted his attention from the arithmetic of the election to the challenges of governing. He began to select a cabinet, or group of advisers, and to write an inaugural address. But congressional Democrats still held a card in the high-stakes electoral game.

Congress had to sign off on the presidential results before inauguration day on March 5, 1877. Angry Democrats were threatening to block the final vote. Republicans were nearly desperate to gain the cooperation of southern Democrats. At the same time, some Democratic leaders saw a chance to make a deal. Everyone involved knew that if Tilden was elected, he would remove all federal troops from the South. Southern Democrats wanted the same commitment from

Hayes. In a private meeting, Republican leaders agreed to this request. They also agreed to Democratic demands that Hayes appoint a southerner to his cabinet and provide federal funds to rebuild the South.

Hayes did not negotiate personally with southern Democrats or make any formal commitments to them. However, the understandings reached between his Republican friends and the Democrats were agreeable to him. With these understandings as background, the Democrats gave up their fight. They allowed Congress to take a final vote at 4:10 A.M. on Friday, March 2, 1877. Shortly afterward, as Hayes wrote in his diary, "we were wakened to hear the news . . . that I was declared elected!"

———————————— ✧ ————————————

The Electoral Commission set up to decide whether Hayes or Tilden would become president announces its decision in March 1877.

XI.—No. 1056.]   NEW YORK, SATURDAY, MARCH 24, 1877.   [WITH A S
PRICE T

Entered according to Act of Congress, in the Year 1877, by Harper & Brothers, in the Office of the Librarian of Congress, at Washington.

Hayes takes the presidential oath of office on March 5, 1877. Chief Justice Morrison R. Waite administered the oath of office, both at Hayes's private inauguration on March 3 and at his public inauguration, shown here.

CHAPTER SEVEN

PRESIDENT HAYES

I now hope for peace, and what is equally important, security and prosperity for the colored [African American] people.
—Rutherford Hayes, on the end of Reconstruction, in a diary entry, April 22, 1877

The formal presidential inauguration was set for Monday, March 5, 1877. President Grant advised Hayes to take the oath of office earlier, in case any problems arose in the public ceremony. (Hayes had received death threats during the election controversy.) So the chief justice of the United States swore Hayes in as the new president in a private ceremony at the White House on Saturday, March 3. Two days later, in front of the U.S. Capitol, Hayes took the oath of office again. Thirty thousand spectators dressed for the cold, cloudy weather attended.

In his inaugural address, Hayes said that "the time has come" for the southern states to govern themselves without

*Fireworks light up the sky on the evening of Hayes's
1877 presidential inauguration.*

a federal military presence. But, he added, "it must be a government which guards the interests of both races carefully and equally." Hayes urged the states, southern and northern, to create more public schools for citizens of both races. Education, he believed, would lead to greater well-being for all Americans.

The new president concluded his speech by referring to the election controversy. "Upon one point there is entire unanimity [agreement] in public sentiment—that conflicting claims to the Presidency must be . . . peaceably adjusted," he said positively.

COMPROMISE OR BETRAYAL?

Hayes was overly optimistic in suggesting that those who opposed his election would set aside their arguments. Democratic newspapers dubbed him His Fraudulency and Rutherfraud. Across the country, Democrats insisted that Hayes had robbed Samuel Tilden of the presidency.

Hayes was also unrealistically optimistic about the South. Although he had supported radical Reconstruction, he believed the time had come to move on. Among white southerners, Reconstruction governments and northern troops had stirred up intense hatred against African Americans, Republicans, and northerners. Hayes thought that hatred would turn to cooperation if southern whites felt in control of their own destinies. He chose to believe promises they made to obey the Fourteenth and Fifteenth amendments. Hayes envisioned a South in which black and whites would share political power.

Hayes had these considerations in mind—as well as the promises his supporters had made to southern Democrats during the election crisis—in April 1877. That month he ordered the withdrawal of the few federal troops that still remained in the South. Reconstruction was officially over.

Hayes was hopeful, as ever. He wrote in his diary, "The result of my plans is . . . that the colored people shall have equal rights to labor, education, and the privileges of citizenship. I am confident this is a good work. Time will tell."

Time did, indeed, tell the story. Hayes had good intentions, but white supremacists in the South did not. With federal troops gone, white southerners quickly took over in Louisiana, South Carolina, and Florida. They tightened their grip on the rest of the former Confederacy. They did not, as Hayes had hoped, show any interest in sharing power with black citizens. Using violence and fraud, they kept blacks from voting. All-white legislatures passed laws stripping black citizens of political power. White leaders barred black Americans from public facilities such as schools, railroads, hotels, and restaurants. Some whites called the withdrawal of troops from the South the Compromise of 1877. Black people and others who favored equal rights called it the Great Betrayal.

Hayes maintained his positive outlook. But he was aware that the nation's race problem would not be easily fixed. He appointed abolitionist (antislavery activist) Frederick Douglass to the position of U.S. marshal for Washington, D.C. This was the highest U.S. government post ever held by any African American at the time. But the appointment caused great opposition among whites in

the nation's capital. Hayes reached out to southerners, such as by including a former Confederate in his cabinet as postmaster general. Radical Republicans then criticized him for being too friendly with the South.

✧ ——————————

In 1877 Frederick Douglass became the first African American to hold the post of U.S marshall.

CLEANING UP GOVERNMENT

In matters other than race relations, Hayes also found himself angering Republicans as much as Democrats. First, he tried to reform civil service. Often during this era, officeholders awarded jobs to party loyalists, especially those who had given them large campaign contributions or even bribes. Hayes wanted government jobs filled on the basis of jobseekers' qualifications instead. But his efforts to reform the civil service displeased some Republicans who enjoyed the benefits of bribes and political favors.

A main target of Hayes's efforts was the U.S. Custom House in New York City. Custom houses collected fees on goods imported from foreign countries. New York City was a major port for imports. So the New York Custom House took in 70 percent of the money the nation collected from customs fees. For years, Republican New York senator Roscoe Conkling had controlled the Custom House. Conkling handed out Custom House jobs to friends and supporters. They paid fees to Conkling's New York Republican organization. Custom House employees worked leisurely hours and pledged strict loyalty to Conkling.

Roscoe Conkling
——— ✧ ———

Conkling's top employees at the Custom House (including New York port collector Chester A. Arthur) refused to change their ways. So Hayes tried to fire them and replace them with his own reform-minded officials. In the Senate, Conkling blocked Hayes's appointments and denounced the president.

This political cartoon shows President Hayes (center), Treasury Secretary Sherman (left), and Secretary of State Evarts (right) attempting to hold up the New York Custom House while Conkling sits on the roof. He holds a victory flag because he had just been reelected to the U.S. Senate.

✧ —————————————

Hayes finally won the standoff in late 1878, with the help of congressional Democrats who were happy to vote against Conkling. Hayes's victory struck a blow for the power of the presidency, which had been weakened by President Grant's reputation for corruption and President Johnson's conflicts with Congress over Reconstruction. Hayes stood up for the right of the president to shape the presidential departments according to his policies. He did not believe a president should have to follow the demands of legislators such as Senator Conkling. But the victory came at a cost. The feud between Conkling and Hayes divided the Republican Party.

MONEY POLICY

Even if the Republican Party had been united behind him, Hayes would have faced difficulty carrying out his policies. For the first two years of his term, Democrats held a majority in the House of Representatives. In the 1878 congressional elections, Democrats took control of the Senate as well. The Republican president could accomplish very little without wrangling with Congress.

For example, Hayes held strong views on the nation's economy, which still suffered from the aftermath of the Panic of 1873. He believed the key to a strong economy was a gold-standard currency. That is, he thought the government should create only as much paper money as it had gold in its bank vaults. In recent years, the government had issued paper money called greenbacks. Yet the government did not have a matching amount of gold in the government treasury. Hayes believed this policy led to paper money that was worth less than its stated value. This could lead people to lose confidence in the nation's money supply.

Congress favored a more lenient standard for issuing money than Hayes did. Limiting the money supply to match gold in the government's possession would mean less money in circulation. Many Americans feared this limit would make it harder for farmers and businesspeople to borrow money. Responding to these concerns, Congress passed the Bland-Allison Act in 1878 . This measure committed the government to issuing silver dollars that were not tied to the gold supply. In Hayes's view, this process was the same as issuing greenbacks not backed by gold. He vetoed the law. Congress had enough votes to override the veto, and Bland-Allison became law.

Still, Hayes managed to accomplish some of his money goals. During his administration, the government made purchases of gold to increase the amount held by the U.S. Treasury. As a result, Hayes was able to have the government print paper money that was backed by gold after all.

This political cartoon about the passage of the Bland-Allison Act is called "Congress Puts Its Foot Down." It represents Congress overriding Hayes's veto of the act. The foot (Congress) is squashing some of the Congressmen who did not support the act.

TAKING THE LEAD

Despite a mostly uncooperative Congress and difficulty with his own Republican Party, Hayes managed to chalk up some accomplishments. Responding to racist feelings in the West, Congress passed a bill in 1878 to bar Chinese immigrants from coming to the United States. The bill violated a treaty the United States had with China, and Hayes vetoed it. (He later negotiated a new treaty with China. In this treaty, the Chinese government agreed to limit immigration to the United States in exchange for a U.S. commitment to buy more Chinese-made goods.)

In foreign affairs, Hayes took a firm stance toward Mexican citizens who entered U.S. territory to steal cattle and other property. He authorized U.S. troops to pursue the raiders back into Mexican territory. But Hayes's political opponents accused him of trying to start a war with Mexico. In fact, neither Hayes nor Mexico's president, Porfirio Díaz, was interested in war. The two nations settled the border problem peaceably.

Not all of President Hayes's accomplishments were worthy of praise. Early in his term, railroad, coal, and other workers across the country walked off their jobs to protest low pay and long hours. The workers' action, known as the Great Strike of 1877, infuriated business leaders and worried state officials. Hayes expressed sympathy for the laborers, but his actions told a different story. He sent federal troops to forcibly put down the workers' demonstrations and riots.

Hayes also did not stop the government's long-standing practices of forcing Native Americans off their lands. The Crow and Blackfoot in Montana, the Ute in Colorado, and the Nez Perce in Idaho were all crushed by American westward expansion during the Hayes administration.

LIFE IN THE WHITE HOUSE

Hayes had an orderly approach to the responsibilities of the presidency. He arose at 7:00 in the morning. Early hours were taken up with writing, breakfast, and family Bible readings. Afterward, Hayes worked, received callers, or met with his cabinet. After lunch, he wrote letters and other papers until taking a carriage ride at 3:30 P.M. After the ride, he sometimes took a short nap, followed by dinner and then a reception for visitors until 10:30 or 11:00 P.M. Hayes tried to make time for physical activity. He exercised before he got dressed, took short brisk walks after meals, and went horseback riding.

He also continued to travel extensively. Early in his term, he went north to Massachusetts and Vermont and south to Kentucky, Tennessee, Georgia, and Virginia. Later, he visited Gettysburg, Pennsylvania, and sailed the Hudson River in New York. He traveled to Chicago, Illinois, and Saint Paul, Minnesota. Tours of Ohio, Michigan, Kansas, Illinois, and Indiana followed.

While home at the White House, President and First Lady Hayes brought their own style to the capital's social scene. They were a family-oriented, informal couple. This style was reflected in much of their entertaining. Early in his administration, after a state dinner at which some of the guests got drunk, Hayes decided to ban liquor from the White House. In this, Hayes was following the lead of his wife, who did not drink alcohol. Many members of the public jeered the unfashionable decision, blaming Lemonade Lucy, as they called the First Lady. Hayes drank alcohol in moderation, but he wanted to set an example with this decision.

WHITE HOUSE FIRSTS

President and First Lady Lucy Webb Hayes marked several milestones in the history of the presidency. The first White House telephone was installed during Hayes's term. Hayes was the first president to have a typewriter in the White House, and the first president to have official correspondence written by typewriter. Lucy Webb Hayes was the first president's wife to graduate from college. And Lucy Webb Hayes was the first First Lady to be called . . . First Lady.

This sketch shows Lucy's popular Sunday night sing-alongs at the White House. Friends of the Hayeses', members of Congress, and other visitors joined together each Sunday evening to sing gospel and folk songs.

———————————————— ♦ ————————————————

Even without alcohol at the White House, social events there were lively. Lucy became known as a wonderful hostess. One newspaper called her "the life and soul of any party." She hosted informal sing-alongs on Sunday evenings (having a very good voice herself). The two younger Hayes children, Scott and Fanny (who were nine and twelve years old in 1880), lived in the White House and had a grand time. They especially loved holiday and birthday parties. Their mother began the tradition of holding an Easter egg roll on the White House lawn.

PROTECTING PRESIDENTIAL POWER

During the second half of his four-year term as president, Hayes continued struggling with the Democratic Congress.

Hayes's children Scott and Fanny, during their years at the White House
✧ ——————————

In 1879 and 1880, southern Democrats in Congress wanted to get rid of Civil War-era and Reconstruction-era laws that allowed federal judges to appoint election supervisors and marshals to protect citizens' right to vote. With these changes, Democrats hoped to further weaken the rights of black citizens. The Democrats attached these measures to bills concerning completely unrelated issues—bills that Hayes wanted to see passed. Democrats hoped that Hayes would sign the bills, even though they contained racist provisions. But Hayes vetoed the Democratic bills over and over again. His firm yet calm stance on these principles earned him widespread approval.

Many Republicans, in fact, wanted Hayes to give up his pledge not to seek a second term as president. But Hayes did not even consider changing his mind. By 1880 he was more than ready to leave office. "I am now in my last year of the Presidency," he wrote to his Texas friend Guy Bryan, "and look forward to its close as a schoolboy longs for the coming vacation."

PRAISED IN PARAGUAY

One can search a map of Hayes's beloved home state of Ohio in vain looking for a town or county named after him. But look at a map of Paraguay (below), and you'll find not only a town but also a whole department—the equivalent of a state—honoring Rutherford B. Hayes. Yet Hayes never visited the South American nation. He had no family relationship to Paraguay. He did not conclude an important treaty with the country. What did he do to deserve such a distinction?

During Hayes's presidency, Paraguay and its neighbor Argentina were involved in a dispute over a large parcel of land that lay on the border between the two nations. They asked Hayes to serve as the arbitrator, or judge, between their competing claims. After reviewing the arguments and evidence from both sides, Hayes decided in late 1878 that the land in question rightfully belonged to Paraguay.

In gratitude, the Paraguayan government named a department (that included the land at the center of the dispute) after the U.S. president, calling it Presidente Hayes. The capital of the department was called Villa Hayes.

Lucy and Rutherford Hayes were relieved to be leaving the White House in 1880.

CHAPTER EIGHT

"THE APPROPRIATE WORK OF PEACE"

To perpetuate the Union and to abolish slavery were the work of war. To educate the uneducated is the appropriate work of peace.
—Rutherford Hayes, summer 1880

In June 1880, Republicans settled on James Garfield as their candidate for the November presidential election. For vice president, the Republicans nominated Chester Arthur. (Hayes had fired him from his position as collector of the port of New York three years before.) Despite his earlier disagreement with Arthur, Hayes backed the Republican ticket. He met privately with Garfield, a fellow Ohioan, to offer encouragement.

With his term coming to a close, Hayes decided to make one more presidential tour. With family members and friends, he set out by train for California on September 1, 1880. The party of travelers made frequent

President and First Lady Hayes are photographed at Yosemite National Park in California during their 1880 tour of the West.

stops along the way, and Hayes met local dignitaries and made speeches. Upon reaching San Francisco, California, Hayes became the first president to visit the country's West Coast while in office.

When the travelers came to the end of the railroad line in northern California, they transferred to stagecoach and headed to Oregon. "What a beautiful country we have passed through," Lucy wrote, "what magnificent scenery grand majestic trees and of fruits the most luscious I ever tasted." In Washington Territory, Hayes and his party toured the scenic Columbia River and Puget Sound.

In late October, the party headed home. They reached Hayes's home in Fremont, Ohio, early on the morning of November 1, 1880. The trip had cost Hayes $575.40, which he paid out of his own pocket, as the government did not pay for such expenses in those days. Hayes pronounced his expedition a success: "Our trip was most fortunate in all of its circumstances," he recorded in his diary. "Superb weather, good health, and no accidents."

WRAPPING UP

Hayes cast his vote in Ohio for Garfield, who won the presidency over the Democratic candidate, General Winfield Scott Hancock. Happy with Garfield's victory, Hayes returned to Washington for the final months of his term.

Much of Hayes's time in his last months in office was occupied with Native American policy. He focused on providing compensation (payment) to Ponca Indians, whom the U.S. government had forced from their traditional lands in Nebraska in 1877. He also had to make appointments, including the appointment of a new justice to the Supreme Court. These were difficult matters and no doubt contributed to Hayes's eagerness to return to private life. Still, he wrote on New Year's Day 1881, "Nobody ever left the Presidency with less regret, less disappointment, fewer heartburnings, or more general content with the result of his term (in his own heart, I mean), than I do."

On March 4, James Garfield was inaugurated as the twentieth president. By the next day, Hayes and his family were on a train bound for Ohio. Near Baltimore, the train was involved in a serious accident, resulting in the deaths of two people. Neither Hayes nor anyone in his family was injured, but the collision was frightening. After some delay in Baltimore, the Hayes party continued their voyage on a different train. They were met in Fremont by crowds of people welcoming them home.

COMMUNITY ACTIVIST

At the age of fifty-eight, the former president was young and healthy enough to enjoy his retirement. He took regular outdoor exercise, walking six miles a day around the lands of Spiegel Grove. "Weighed at butcher's on Croghan street," he wrote in his diary soon after his return to Ohio, "one hundred and ninety-two [pounds]. Told the young man I must walk off five pounds."

On their estate, Hayes and Lucy kept farm animals such as chickens, which Lucy enjoyed tending. They added several dogs to their household. A Newfoundland named Hector, a terrier named Dot, and a greyhound named Grim all enjoyed the family's love and attention.

Hayes quickly became involved in community work in Fremont. He joined the governing boards of the Birchard Library (established by his uncle), Western Reserve University, Ohio State University, Ohio Wesleyan University, and a local school, cemetery, and bank. Ever proud of his Civil War service, he belonged to a variety of military groups. Reaching out beyond his community and Ohio, Hayes remained involved in the cause of prison reform, which he had embraced while governor. He spoke tirelessly of the need for humane prison conditions.

Among the many organizations with which he was involved, closest to Hayes's heart were two whose goals matched his own. One was the Peabody Education Fund, whose mission was the improvement of overall education in the South. The other was the Slater Fund, devoted to the education of black southerners in particular. In his optimistic way, Hayes firmly believed that greater educational achievement by blacks as well as whites would help erase the differences and strife between the races. At the same time, he recognized that the nation was far from solving its race problem, whether in the North or South. "Certain it is," he wrote in a letter to Benjamin Tucker Tanner, a black minister and educator, "the people of the North have not in the last six years made greater progress in getting away from barbarism [cruelty or brutality] in the treatment of the colored man than the people of the South have made in the same period. . . . We are all to blame in this matter."

Hayes continued to travel. He frequently visited New York City, where both the Peabody and Slater funds were headquartered. He also visited friends and gave speeches throughout the Midwest, East, and South. Lucy was often his companion on these trips.

AN "EXCEPTIONALLY HAPPY" LIFE

Lucy began having health problem in 1883. She suffered from painful abdominal attacks, possibly a result of a gall bladder disease. When she felt well enough, however, Lucy continued to shape a lively social life at Spiegel Grove, hosting musical events and other parties. Their children lived away most of the time. Fanny and Scott were in

The Hayes family poses at their home in Ohio in 1887. From left to right are Birch, his wife Mary, Hayes, Scott, Rutherford, Lucy, Fanny, and Webb.

————————— ◇ —————————

school, Rud was in college, and Webb and Birch were pursuing careers. They sometimes came home on weekends and other occasions. Hayes and Lucy became grandparents in 1887 when Birch and his wife had a son, whom they named Rutherford.

Sadness intruded into Hayes's contentment. Several good friends died, including Stanley Matthews. Hayes had volunteered for the Twenty-third Regiment with him years earlier. Matthew went on to become a Supreme Court justice. Even closer to home, young Rutherford, the Hayes's grandson, died in late 1888. He was less than fourteen months old.

Hayes enjoyed almost forty years with his beloved Lucy before she died of a stroke in 1889.
——————— ✧

For Hayes, the worst was yet to come. In late June 1889, Hayes returned to Fremont after a brief trip to Columbus. Waiting for him at the train station was his son Rud, bearing the news that Lucy had suffered a paralyzing stroke while sitting at her bedroom window sewing. A few days later, Lucy died at home in the bedroom with Hayes at her side. She was two months away from her fifty-eighth birthday.

Lucy had been Hayes's best friend, and he felt her loss deeply. A few months later, on his birthday, he wrote in his diary, "My birthday—sixty-seven. It brings freshly and painfully to mind the absence from my side of my cherished Lucy. . . . Alas, how it weakens the hold of this life—of earth upon me! How easily I could now let go of life!"

Love Letters of Rutherford B. Hayes

For thirty-eight years, Rutherford and Lucy Hayes shared the type of love that valentines are made of. Hayes was a letter writer, and from the day they were engaged in 1851, Hayes revealed his heart and mind to Lucy in his writings.

"[H]ereafter with you I mean to think aloud," he wrote to Lucy a week after their engagement, "and I wish you to do the same with me. If we are to spend our lives with and for each other, the more intimately and thoroughly we understand each other the better each will be able to please the other." "Tell me anything—everything, how you feel," he wrote her in August 1851. "Let me see your heart. God knows I love you as my life, and shall ever."

As years went by, Hayes loved his wife more and more, and he continued to pour out his feelings in letters. During his service in the Civil War, Hayes's letters home were full of love and longing for his wife. In one war letter, he expressed a new measurement of his love: "I think of you and the boys oftener than ever. Love to 'em and *oceans* for yourself."

✧ ————————

The Hayses exchanged many love letters through the years. This one was written by Lucy while Hayes was fighting in the Civil War.

The Hayes gave each other jewelry on their twenty-fifth wedding anniversary in 1877. A brooch (left) that Hayes gave to Lucy has his image on it. Cufflinks (one is shown, right) that Lucy gave to Hayes bear her image.

——————— ✧ ———————

Hayes also savored and celebrated his love privately, in his diary. His journal entry of December 30, 1872, reads: "Our wedding day, twenty years ago! A happy day. Darling is handsomer than she was then, with a glorious flow of friendly feeling and cheerfulness, genuine womanly character, a most affectionate mother, a good, good wife. How I do love her! What a lucky man I was and am!" Eight years later, Hayes's ardor had not faded a bit. Celebrating Lucy's forty-ninth birthday in 1880, he wrote, "Lucy is forty-nine today. I never loved her so much as now."

When Lucy died in 1889, Hayes was heartbroken. He missed her deeply for the remaining four years of his life. As he lay dying in 1893, his last words were, "I know that I am going where Lucy is."

This photograph was taken after Lucy's death in 1889. Pictured from left to right are Hayes's son Rutherford, Lucy Herron (a friend of the family), Hayes himself, and his daughter, Fanny.

——————————— ◇ ———————————

Hayes did not let go of life, but his thoughts were rarely far from his wife and soul mate. He continued to travel (always bringing photographs of Lucy with him to set out in his hotel rooms). In April 1890, he and his daughter, Fanny, took a sea voyage from New York to Bermuda, a British island in the Atlantic Ocean. He enjoyed the island's weather and natural beauty and called the home where he and Fanny stayed a paradise. He wrote, "I wept to think that Lucy never saw it."

Although life no longer had the spark it once had, Hayes did not neglect his commitments. In 1890 and

1892, he spoke at conferences that addressed what was then called the Negro question—the ongoing problems of black Americans and racial prejudice. He visited southern schools as part of his work with the Slater Fund to provide educational support for black Americans.

But Hayes was not as robust as he once had been. He found traveling more wearying than in the past, and he was prone to stomach upsets and colds. Still, after every recovery came another trip for him. He traveled to Washington, D.C., for a large gathering of Civil War veterans in September 1892. The next month, after celebrating his seventieth birthday at home with family, he was on the road again for meetings and a conference in New York. He enjoyed the winter holidays with his family at Spiegel Grove. January 1893 brought snow and, as Hayes noted in his diary, "great sleighing!"

Hayes went to Columbus and Cleveland in mid-January. On the train back from Cleveland to Fremont, he felt unusually cold and then experienced severe chest pains, the sign of a heart attack. Hayes made it home to Spiegel Grove, where his doctor ordered him to bed. He stayed in bed for three days and was well enough at one point to joke with a cousin who was taking care of him. But Hayes felt the end was near. "I am not unhappy," he said. "My life is an exceptionally happy one." Three days after his heart attack on the train, on January 17, 1893, Hayes died.

LEGACY OF DECENCY

By the time of his death, many Americans admired Hayes. They welcomed his efforts to reform the civil service. They

A long procession of mourners, led by military units, filed from Spiegel Grove to the cemetery for Hayes's funeral in 1893. His casket was carried by his Civil War comrades.

————————————— ◇ —————————————

championed the way Hayes stood up to members of Congress—both antireform Republicans such as Roscoe Conkling and anti–Fifteenth Amendment Democrats. Admirers viewed his removal of federal troops from southern capitals as necessary to reducing hostility between North and South.

Later generations have been less kind in evaluating the nineteenth president. For instance, critics point out that Hayes talked more about civil service reform than he actually accomplished. The gold-backed money that Hayes embraced was viewed as an old-fashioned notion and bad economic policy in the twentieth century and was abandoned. (Although the nation has gold reserves, the U.S. money supply is not tied to those reserves.) And Hayes did not differ from most other presidents in allowing the government to grab land from Native Americans and to resettle Native Americans onto reservations, with no regard for their culture.

In his monetary and Indian policy, Hayes was very much a man of the 1880s and 1890s. He was a thoughtful person, but not ahead of his times. In his southern policy, Hayes was in some ways trapped by circumstances existing at the time of his election. The North had tired of supporting southern Reconstruction governments with an expensive army. And, the South was in turmoil because of racist whites determined to oppress the newly freed slaves. Hayes was also the victim of his own optimistic personality. He truly believed that good white people would rise to leadership in the South and share power with black Americans. That, of course, did not happen during his presidency.

What was most notable and admirable about Hayes— both as president and as a private citizen—was his basic human decency. If in 1877 he was overly optimistic about the behavior of southern whites toward black Americans, this was because he assumed more people would behave as he did. For Hayes, decency, compassion, and respect of others came naturally. So did the ability to laugh at himself. Throughout his life, Hayes also had the ability to enjoy what the world offered and to cherish his friends and family, especially his adored Lucy. His greatest achievement was not his presidency. It was his ability to live a life full of experience, effort, morality, and love.

Timeline

1817   Sophia and Rutherford Hayes move from Vermont to central Ohio.

1822   Rutherford Birchard Hayes is born in Delaware, Ohio, on October 4.

1825   Hayes's older brother, Lorenzo, dies at the age of nine.

1834   Hayes and his family travel to New England to visit relatives.

1836   Hayes attends Norwalk Seminary, a boarding school in Norwalk, Ohio.

1837   Hayes attends Isaac Webb's Preparatory School in Middletown, Connecticut.

1838   Hayes enrolls in Kenyon College in Gambier, Ohio, in November.

1842   Hayes graduates from Kenyon College and studies law at a firm in Columbus, Ohio.

1843   Hayes enters Harvard Law School in Cambridge, Massachusetts.

1845   Hayes graduates from Harvard Law School and moves to Lower Sandusky, Ohio, where he establishes a law practice.

1847   Hayes meets Lucy Ware Webb, a college student from Chillicothe, Ohio.

1848   With his uncle, Sardis Birchard, Hayes travels to Texas to visit former schoolmate Guy Bryan.

1849   On Christmas Eve, Hayes moves to Cincinnati, where he sets up a new law practice.

1852 In February, Hayes serves as defense attorney for accused murderer Nancy Farrer. His work in that case helps cement his reputation as an up-and-coming lawyer. On December 30, Hayes marries Lucy Ware Webb.

1853 Lucy gives birth to the Hayeses' first child, a boy named Birchard. Hayes and other Cincinnati attorneys form the law firm of Corwine, Hayes and Rogers.

1855 Hayes participates in the formation of the Republican Party in Ohio.

1856 A second son, Webb, is born in March. Hayes's beloved sister, Fanny, dies in July.

1858 A third son, named Rutherford, is born in June. In December Hayes becomes the city solicitor (lawyer) of Cincinnati.

1860 Abraham Lincoln is elected as sixteenth president of the United States. In response, South Carolina becomes the first of eleven states to secede from the Union and form the Confederacy.

1861 The Civil War begins. Hayes joins the Union army, as part of the Twenty-third Ohio Regiment. In September Hayes engages in battle at Carnifex Ferry in western Virginia.

1862 Hayes's regiment participates in the Battle of South Mountain in Maryland. Union forces are victorious in the engagement, but Hayes is seriously wounded.

1863 The Hayeses' baby son, Joseph, dies during a family reunion in West Virginia.

1864 While Hayes is fighting in the Shenandoah Valley of Virginia, the citizens of Cincinnati elect him as their representative to the U.S. Congress. Lucy gives birth to a fifth son, George.

1865 The Civil War ends in April. In November Hayes takes his seat as a U.S. congressman in Washington, D.C.

1866 Congressman Hayes votes in support of Reconstruction policies. The Hayeses' youngest son, George, dies. Hayes wins reelection to Congress.

1867 Lucy gives birth to a sixth child, a girl named Fanny. Hayes is elected governor of Ohio.

1869 The people of Ohio reelect Hayes to a second term as governor.

1870 With Hayes's support, the Ohio legislature ratifies the Fifteenth Amendment to the U.S. Constitution.

1871 A seventh child, a son named Scott, is born in February.

1872 Hayes retires as governor. At the urging of Ohio Republicans, he runs for Congress and loses.

1873 Hayes and his family move to Fremont, Ohio, to live at Spiegel Grove. In August Lucy gives birth to an eighth child, a boy named Manning.

1874 Hayes's Uncle Sardis dies in January, followed by the death of son Manning in August.

1875 Hayes runs for and wins a third term as governor of Ohio.

1876 Hayes is nominated as the Republican Party's candidate for president. The election results are uncertain, leading to months of conflict and debate between the Republicans and Democrats.

1877 On March 2, Congress names Hayes winner of the 1876 presidential election. Hayes is inaugurated as the nineteenth president. Reconstruction ends with the removal of federal troops from southern capitals.

1878 Hayes reduces corruption in the New York Custom House.

1880 Hayes travels to the western United States, becoming the first president to visit California while in office.

1881 James Garfield is inaugurated as the twentieth president. Hayes and his family return to Fremont, Ohio, to live at Spiegel Grove.

1889 Lucy Hayes dies in June.

1893 On January 17, Rutherford B. Hayes dies at the age of seventy.

SOURCE NOTES

7 Rutherford Birchard Hayes, *Diary and Letters of Rutherford Birchard Hayes, Nineteenth President of the United States* ed. Charles Richard Williams, 5 vols. (Columbus: The Ohio State Archaeological and Historical Society, 1922–1926), diary entry, November 11, 1876, http://www.ohiohistory.org/onlinedoc/hayes/ (December 10, 2005).

7 Ibid.

8 Ari Hoogenboom, *Rutherford B. Hayes: Warrior and President* (Lawrence, KS: University Press of Kansas, 1995), 274.

9 Hayes, letter, June 21, 1836.

12 Ibid. n.d. entry, chap. 1.

12 Ibid.

13 Ibid.

14 Hayes, "Rutherford B. Hayes Journal of Summer 1834," chap. 1.

15 Hoogenboom, 21.

17 Hans L. Trefousse, *Rutherford B. Hayes* (New York: Henry Holt and Company, 2002), 5.

17–18 Hayes, letter, December 9, 1838.

18 Ibid., letter, February 24, 1838.

19 Ibid., letter, February 5, 1839.

20–21 Ibid., diary entry, February 10, 1841.

21 Ibid., diary entry, June 19, 1841.

21 Ibid.

22 Ibid., letter, January 31, 1842.

23 Ibid., n.d., letter, chap. 5.

25 Ibid., letter, January 1, 1845.

27 Ibid., letter, October 23, 1847.

27 Ibid., letter, August 20, 1846.

28 Ibid., diary entry, January 25, 1849.

28 Ibid.

28 Ibid., letter, January 27, 1849.

30 Trefousse, 10.

31 Rutherford B. Hayes Presidential Center, "Memorable Quotes from the Diary and Letters of Rutherford B. Hayes," 2005, http://www.ohiohistory.org/onlinedoc/hayes/quotes.html (December 10, 2005).

33 Trefousse, 16.

35 Hayes, diary entry, January 27, 1861.

37 Ibid., diary entry, May 15, 1861.

37 Ibid.

38 Ibid., letter, June 14, 1861.

38 Ibid., letter, July 27, 1861.

38 Ibid., diary entry, September 10, 1861.

39–40 Ibid., diary entry, January 15, 1861.

40 Ibid., diary entry, May 1, 1862.

40 Ibid., diary entry, May 11, 1862.

42 Ibid., diary entry, September 18, 1862.

42 Ibid., letter, September 15, 1862.

43 Ibid., letter, March 10, 1839.

43 Ibid., diary entry, November 24, 1857.

43 Ibid., letter, September 16, 1862.

46 Ibid., diary entry, June 12, 1864.

46 Ibid., letter, July 2, 1864.

46 Rutherford B. Hayes Presidential Center, "Memorable Quotes."

49 Hayes, letter, April 16, 1865.

51 Hoogenboom, 212–213.

56 Hayes, letter, October 9, 1867.

57 Ibid., letter, January 17, 1868.

59 Ibid., letter, January 9, 1872.

62 Ibid., diary entries, March 18 and 20, 1875.
63 Hoogenboom, 260.
65 Hayes, letter, December 6, 1876.
68 Jeff Greenfield, "Hayes's Ride," *Washington Monthly*, March 2003, http://www .washingtonmonthly.com/ features/2003/0303.greenfield .html (December 10, 2005).
68 Hayes, letter, October 5, 1876.
70 Ibid., letter, November 27, 1876.
73 Ibid., diary entry, March 14, 1877.
75 Ibid., diary entry, April 22, 1877.
75–76 Avalon Project at Yale Law School, "Inaugural Address of Rutherford B. Hayes," *Avalon Project*, 1997, http://www.yale.edu/lawweb/ avalon/presiden/inaug/hayes .htm (December 10, 2005).
77 Hayes, diary entry, April 22, 1877.
85 Miller Center of Public Affairs, "Rutherford Birchard Hayes," *AmericanPresident .org*, 2003, http://www .americanpresident.org/ history/rutherfordbhayes/ biography/FamilyLife .common.shtml (December 10, 2005).
86 Trefousse, 118–119.
89 Rutherford B. Hayes Presidential Center, "Memorable Quotes."
90 Hoogenboom, 443.
91 Hayes, diary entry, November 7, 1880.
91 Ibid., letter, January 1, 1881.
92 Ibid., diary entry, March 11, 1881.
93 Ibid., letter, February 20, 1883.
95 Rutherford B. Hayes Presidential Center. "Memorable Quotes."
96 Hayes, letter, June 22, 1851.
96 Ibid., letter, August 10, 1851.
96 Ibid., letter, April 5, 1863.
97 Ibid., diary entry, December 30, 1872.
97 Ibid., diary entry, August 28, 1880.
97 Trefousse, 146.
98 Hayes, diary entry, April 20, 1890.
99 Hoogenboom, 531.
99 Ibid., 532.

Selected Bibliography

Foner, Eric. *Reconstruction, 1863–1877.* New York: Harper & Row, 1988.

Hoogenboom, Ari. *Rutherford B. Hayes, Warrior and President.* Lawrence, KS: University Press of Kansas, 1995.

Rutherford B. Hayes Presidential Center. *Rutherford B. Hayes: Citizen, Soldier, President* (CD-ROM). Fremont, OH: Legacy Publishing, 1999.

Rutherford B. Hayes Presidential Center Website. http://www.rbhayes.org.

Trefousse, Hans L. *Rutherford B. Hayes.* New York: Henry Holt and Company, 2002.

Ward, Geoffrey C. *The Civil War: An Illustrated History.* New York: Alfred A. Knopf, 1990.

Williams, Charles Richard, ed. *Diary and Letters of Rutherford B. Hayes.* Columbus, Ohio: Ohio State Archeological and Historical Society, 1922. http://www.ohiohistory.org/onlinedoc/hayes.

Further Reading and Websites

American Presidents: Life Portraits
http://www.americanpresidents.org
This website accompanies a C-SPAN television series about the presidents.

Arnold, James R. *The Civil War.* Minneapolis: Lerner Publications Company, 2005.

Feldman, Ruth Tenzer. *James A. Garfield.* Minneapolis: Lerner Publications Company, 2005.

Golay, Michael. *Reconstruction and Reaction: The Emancipation of Slaves, 1861–1913.* New York: Facts on File, Inc., 1996.

Greene, Meg. *Into the Land of Freedom: African Americans in Reconstruction.* Lerner Publications Company, 2004.

Hakim, Joy. *An Age of Extremes.* New York: Oxford University Press, 1999.

———. *Reconstruction and Reform.* New York: Oxford University Press, 1999.

McPherson, James M. *Fields of Fury: The American Civil War.* New York: Atheneum Books for Young Readers, 2002.

Miller Center of Public Affairs, University of Virginia, AmericanPresident.org website, "Rutherford Birchard Hayes." http://www.americanpresident.org/history/rutherfordbhayes/ This detailed website, produced by the University of Virginia's Miller Center of Public Affairs, covers Hayes's entire life and includes links to other sites of interest.

Rutherford B. Hayes Presidential Center. "Lucy Scott West Executive Mansion Journal." http://www.rbhayes.org/mssfind/hayes_coll/westlucy.htm Lucy Scott West was a cousin of First Lady Lucy Webb Hayes, who stayed at the Hayes website for an extended visit in 1878. The journal she kept during her stay, which is reprinted in this website, provides a glimpse of life in Washington, D.C. and in the White House during Hayes's presidency.

INDEX

ABOUT THE AUTHOR

Before she started writing books for children, Debbie Levy worked as a newspaper editor and practiced law with a large Washington, D.C., law firm. She earned a bachelor's degree in government and foreign affairs from the University of Virginia, and a law degree and master's degree in world politics from the University of Michigan. Her previous books include *John Quincy Adams*, *James Monroe*, *Lyndon B. Johnson*, and *The Vietnam War*. Debbie enjoys paddling around in kayaks and canoes and fishing in the Chesapeake Bay region. She lives with her husband, two sons, dog, and cat in Maryland.

--- ◆ ---